D0426539

Tide Pools

by Marcia S. Gresko

KidHaven Press

KidHaven Press, an imprint of Gale Group, Inc.
P.O. Box 289009, San Diego, CA 92198-9009

Library of Congress Cataloging-in-Publication Data
Gresko, Marcia S.
    Tide pools/by Marcia S. Gresko.
       p. cm. — (The kidhaven science library)
    Includes bibliographical references (p.   ).
    Summary: Discusses tides and tide pools and the moon's influ-
    ence on them. The plant and animal life in tide pools is
    described, as well as ecological damage caused by man.
    ISBN 0-7377-0748-8 (hardback : alk. paper)
    1. Tide pool ecology—Juvenile literature. 2. Tide pools—Juvenile
    literature. [1. Tide pools. 2. Tide pool ecology. 3. Ecology.] I. Title.
    II. Series.
    QH541.5.S35 G74 2002
    577.69'9—dc21

    2001001747

Picture Credits:
Cover photo: © Mark Newman
© Biophoto Associates/Photo Researchers, Inc., 15 (bottom)
© Jonathan Blair/CORBIS, 12, 35
© Gary Braasch/CORBIS, 26
Center for Marine Conservation, 38
© Brandon D. Cole/CORBIS, 5
© Jim Corwin/Photo Researchers, Inc., 36
Digital Stock, 9
© Ecoscene/CORBIS, 24, 32
FPG, 14, 39
© Frank Lane Picture Agency/CORBIS, 21
© Darrell Gulin/CORBIS, 15 (top)
© Dave G. Houser/CORBIS, 40
Chris Jouan, 34
© Wolfgang Koehler/CORBIS, 11
© Pat O'Hara/CORBIS, 30, 42
© Stephen P. Parker 1985/Photo Researchers, Inc., 18
© Joel W. Rogers/CORBIS, 20
Martha Schierholz, 6, 7
© Paul A. Souders/CORBIS, 27
© Stuart Westmorland/CORBIS, 17
© Mike Zens/CORBIS, 28

Copyright 2002 by KidHaven Press, an imprint of Gale Group, Inc.
        P. O. Box 289009, San Diego, CA, 92198-9009

No part of this book may be reproduced or used in any other form or
by any other means, electrical, mechanical, or otherwise, including,
but not limited to, photocopying, recording, or any information stor-
age and retrieval system, without prior written permission from the
publisher.

Contents

Tides and Tide Pools

Crabs creep and snails slide. Sea gulls squawk and beach fleas hop. Seaweeds sway, and silvery fish flash among the rocks. Ocean waves swell along the shore. The foaming water invades the beach, swirls among the rocks, and retreats. Gradually, the beach is nearly covered with water. Later, the water moves slowly down the beach again, out to sea. This steady rise and fall of the earth's oceans is called the tide.

Oceans and seas cover more than 70 percent of the earth's surface. All over the planet, wherever the ocean and the shore meet, the tides rise and fall in an unending cycle. Shorelines around the world are different. Most are flat and sandy. Others are low and muddy. Some are covered in coral, ice, or rocks. But along most of the earth's million-plus miles of shoreline, there are two high tides and two low tides each day.

The Tides

Tides are caused by the pull of the earth, moon, and sun on one another. Because the moon is

Creatures in tide pools are affected by the ocean's tides.

closer to the earth than the sun, its **gravity** rules the tides. As the earth turns, the water in the oceans facing the moon is pulled up toward it in a bulge. The water in the oceans on the opposite side of the earth from the moon forms another bulge to balance the planet. These bulges are the high tides. The lowest water levels reached in between the bulges are the low tides.

The sun is much farther away, but its gravity also affects the tides. When the sun, moon, and earth are directly in line with one another (during a new or full moon), the sun helps the moon pull on the ocean. This causes the lowest of low tides and the highest of high tides. Because these tides seem to "spring up from earth," they are called

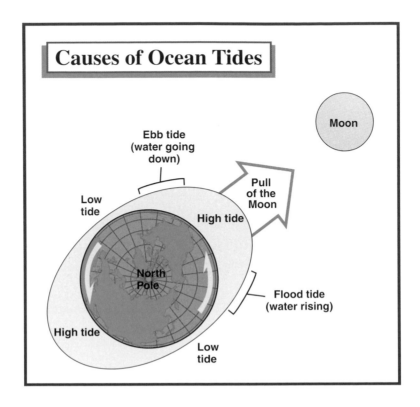

Causes of Ocean Tides

Moon

Ebb tide
(water going
down)

Pull
of the
Moon

Low
tide

High tide

North
Pole

Flood tide
(water rising)

High tide

Low
tide

spring tides. When the sun and moon are not aligned (during first and third quarter phases), their gravitational forces cancel each other out, and the tides are not as dramatically high and low. These tides are called neap tides.

Tide Pools and the Intertidal Zone

A tide pool is made as the waves go out and seawater is trapped in the hollows of rocks and in rocky basins. Tide pools come in all shapes and sizes, and each is different. A tide pool can be round or oval or just a long, jagged, water-filled crack in a rock. A tide pool can be as large as a pond or smaller than a soup bowl, shallow like a puddle or deep like a ditch. A tide pool can be a garden of bright colors or a plain, glassy reflection of the sky.

Tide pools are found in the intertidal zone, the part of the shoreline covered and uncovered by the daily tides. As the tide creeps up the beach, parts of this area are covered for varying lengths of time. Some parts spend most of every day exposed to air and sun. Others remain submerged except during the lowest tides. This creates a series of four main intertidal zones or bands as the shore slopes to the vast, open sea.

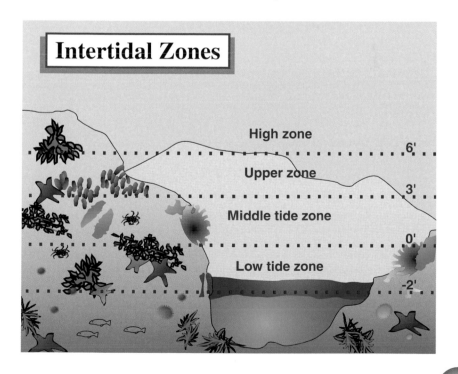

Intertidal Zones

High zone

6'

Upper zone

3'

Middle tide zone

0'

Low tide zone

-2'

Each zone is a special **habitat** shaped by the air, water, and sun. The high zone or "splash zone" is located highest on the shore and seldom covered by the ocean. Since the high zone is watered mostly by salty wave spray and rain, the high zone is dry most of the time. Below the high zone lies the upper zone—sometimes wet, sometimes dry, depending on spring or neap tide conditions. Next is the middle tide zone. Exposed by most low tides and covered by most high tides, it remains dry half the time. Finally, the low tide zone is always underwater except during the lowest low tides. Tide pools are found in all the intertidal zones.

Life in Nature's Aquariums

Tide pools are natural aquariums. They provide homes for peculiar plants and amazing animals. Some of these animals spend their whole life in a tide pool. Others spend part of their life in the ocean. Where a tide pool is located on the shore influences the kinds of plants and animals that live in it. Only a few hardy **species**, such as rough barnacles, shy crabs, and cone-shaped limpets, dwell in the high and upper zone pools. Creatures usually found in the sea itself occupy the low zone pools. Spiny sea urchins, colorful sea slugs, and small fish gather here. The greatest mixture of creatures is found in the middle zone pools.

Besides the regular residents, many animals visit this area to feed as the tide changes. Sleek mussels, slow-moving sea stars, and flowerlike anemones are often seen here.

Life in a tide pool is different from life in the ocean. Conditions change slowly out in the huge ocean. The water temperature stays fairly even. The amount of salt in the water remains stable. Oxygen is constantly being added to the water as the wind whips the waves into a foamy, life-giving froth. Food is plentiful, and there are endless places to hide from hungry hunters. But in the smaller world of the tide pool, conditions change

The greatest variety of sea creatures, like these sea stars, is found in the middle zone pools.

quickly. Tide pool inhabitants face harsh, unpredictable situations and many dangers.

Tide Pool Conditions

Tide pool water temperatures can reach extremes. On warm, sunny days, the water temperature soars. On chilly days and at night, the water temperature plunges. Tide pools can change temperature in seconds, too. After hours of a pool being exposed to the warm sun while the tide is out, creatures can suddenly be exposed to a seventy degree or more drop in temperature when the rising tide splashes back into the pool!

Tide pool oxygen levels can also change quickly. All living things need oxygen to breathe. Warm water does not hold as much oxygen as cool water. As the sizzling sun heats up the tide pool, oxygen bubbles to the surface and escapes into the air. There may not be enough oxygen left for tide pool creatures to breathe, and they can suffocate.

The amount of salt in trapped tide pool water can vary dangerously. Sun and air cause the salty sea water to **evaporate**. When this happens, the water remaining in the tide pool gets even saltier. Tide pool animals may lose water from their bodies, shrivel up, and die. On the other hand, when rain floods the tide pool, the water may not be salty enough. Drenched by too much freshwater, tide pool dwellers can swell up and even burst.

A sun-warmed tide pool can experience a big drop in temperature when the rising tide splashes back into the pool.

Living between hard rocks and pounding surf is another challenge. Four to five waves batter the shore each minute. They strike with crushing force, as much as thousands of pounds of pressure on each square foot of rocky shore. As the waves return to the sea, they tug against the shore, snatching and pulling at the animals and plants clinging to the rocks.

Finally, hungry **predators** make tide pool life a constant struggle. During low tides, watchful sea birds and other land animals study the tide pools hoping to catch a tasty meal. During high tides, ocean animals raid the tide pools for food. There is danger even within the tide pool itself as fierce hunters stalk their gentler neighbors.

Four to five waves crash on the shore each minute.

The tide pool is a miniature world for its **inhabitants**. Despite its many obstacles and challenges, the tide pool remains mostly a peaceful, sheltered place—although nearby the surf may still be pounding away at the shoreline.

Tide Pool Animals

A tide pool is a crowded community filled with unusual animal residents. Some make their homes on or under the jagged rocks. Some live in the swaying seaweeds or in sand or ground-up shells at the bottom of the pool. There are animals everywhere. Most of them are invertebrates—animals without a backbone or spine.

Spiny Skins and Sneaky Stomachs

Echinoderms are the pincushions of the sea. The group's name means "spiny skins." All its members, including sea stars, sea urchins, and sea cucumbers feel bumpy or prickly to the touch.

There are more than two thousand species of sea stars or starfish. Most have five arms, also called rays, but some have as many as fifty. On the tip of each arm is an eyespot for "seeing" and small feelers for "hearing" and "smelling." Hundreds of tube feet on the undersides of the arms help the sea star

Sea stars or starfish usually have five arms equipped with an eyespot, and feelers for "hearing" and "smelling."

move about. If a sea star's arm is broken off, it can grow a new one. A sea star can also regrow itself entirely from just one arm and a small piece of its body. Most echinoderms are **herbivores** (plant-eating animals), but sea stars are predators. They eat everything from small fish to other sea stars, but their favorite dish is mussels. A sea star uses its arms to partly pry open a mussel's shell. Then, the sea star turns its stomach inside out and pushes it through its mouth and into the mussel's shell. After the sea star's stomach digests its meal, the sea star swallows it back again.

The spiky sea urchin is the "porcupine of the sea." Its ball-shaped body is covered with hundreds of sharp spines. Some have poisonous barbs on the ends, which can break off and stick in an attacker. But whenever this happens, the sea urchin just grows new ones. On the urchin's bottom are rows of tube feet and a beaklike mouth with five sharp teeth. As it creeps along, the sea urchin scrapes food from the rocks.

The warty sea cucumber is the strangest echinoderm of all. It looks like the bumpy vegetable sold in the supermarket. Using its tube feet and wormlike movements of its body, the sea cucumber slithers along, squeezing into cracks between rocks, or hiding in a burrow in the sand. From there it sweeps food toward its mouth with its tentacles.

The sea urchin (top) is ball-shaped and covered with hundreds of sharp spikes. The sea cucumber (bottom), named for its similarity to the vegetable, uses tube feet to move around between cracks in rocks.

If it is attacked, the surprising sea cucumber throws its "guts" at the enemy to escape. This would mean death to most animals, but this is just one way the sea cucumber protects itself. It grows a new set of internal organs in a few months.

Mobile Homes and Armored Tents

Some of the most curious-looking creatures in the tide pool are the crustaceans. Crustaceans have jointed legs, two pairs of antennae, and hard, protective shells, but they differ enormously from the scuttling crab to the stationary barnacle.

Moving sideways on four pairs of hairy legs, shy crabs dart about. Called the "garbagemen" of the tide pools, many crabs are scavengers. They eat the remains of dead plants and animals. Others are fierce hunters, using their strong claws to catch and tear apart prey. If a crab loses a claw or leg in a fight, it grows a new one. As they get larger, most crabs also shed their old shells and grow new ones. But hermit crabs do not grow their own shells. Instead, a hermit crab finds the right-sized shell and moves in. If the shell is occupied by another hermit crab, the fearless hermit crab might fight and evict the shell's owner. The hermit crab carries its mobile home along wherever it goes, borrowing or stealing a new one when the old model gets too tight.

Since a hermit crab has no shell, it must find one to use for protection.

Unlike busy crabs, barnacles are homebodies. Once a barnacle finds a rock, or even another tide pool neighbor's shell, it glues itself, head down, to its new home. It grows a sharp, armor-plated tent around its body and stays stuck to the same place for the rest of its life. When the tide comes in, the barnacle opens a trap door and uses its feathery feet to kick bits of food toward its mouth.

Tough Tongues and Bushy Beards

Most of the creatures that live in tide pools are squishy, soft-bodied mollusks. Most mollusks live in shells. One-shelled mollusks, like sea snails and limpets, are called univalves. Mollusks with two shells, like mussels, are called bivalves.

Each species of sea snail has its own kind of shell home. Some are dark and shiny. Others are light, checkered, spotted, or striped. Some are spiral- or cone-shaped. Others are wavy, or shaped like a helmet or turban. A sea snail glides over the rocks on a large, muscular foot. It uses its sandpaper-like tongue, called a radula, to scrape food from the rocks or to drill into other shells to get at the animals inside.

Volcano-shaped limpets are a simple kind of snail. Unlike prowling snails, limpets hang

Blue-black mussels live in colonies, clinging to rocks by strong threads they spin themselves.

around the rocks. A limpet rubs against a rock with its shell to carve a "home base." From there it creeps short distances to graze, returning when the tide goes out. A limpet may use the same snug spot its whole life—ten to fifteen years.

Blue-black mussels gather in **colonies**. They cling to the rocks by strong threads they spin themselves. The threads look like a bushy beard. A mussel can dissolve these threads and move to another part of the tide pool when the colony becomes overcrowded, and then spin new ones. Mussels are filter feeders. They suck water into their shells, strain it for bits of food, and then spit it out.

Peculiar Petals, Funny Fins, and Tiny Drifters

Sea anemones look like underwater flowers, but they are **carnivores** related to jellyfish. Their "petals" are stinging tentacles they use to capture, paralyze, and push small animals into the mouths in the center of their bodies. Sea anemones can move slowly on their thick, stalklike bodies, but most of the time they stay put.

Fish are the tide pool's only vertebrates—animals with a spine. Tide pool fish look different from ocean-dwelling fish. Many are long, smooth, and slippery. Clingfish use suction-cuplike fins to cling to rocks. Worm pipefish have lost almost all their fins. Sand gobies cover themselves in a

Sea anemones are meat-eaters that use stinging tentacles to capture, paralyze, and eat small animals.

pool's sandy bottom with a fin flick. Sea scorpions spread their frilly fins to scare away danger.

Billions of tiny plankton float on the surface of tide pools and the open ocean. Some plankton are eggs or larvae, miniature sea babies that will grow into fish, crabs, sea stars, or barnacles. Most plankton are plantlike organisms. This "sea soup" provides a rich food source for all the animals in the sea. Many animals eat plankton; others eat animals that eat plankton. This is called the food chain.

Iron Grips, Water Savers, and Clever Disguises

Living in a tide pool can be tough. Tide pool animals are survivors. They've learned to adapt to difficult conditions.

When the waves crash, sea stars hold on tightly to the rocks with hundreds of tube feet. Sea

Billions of tiny plankton that float on the surface of seawater are the food source of many animals.

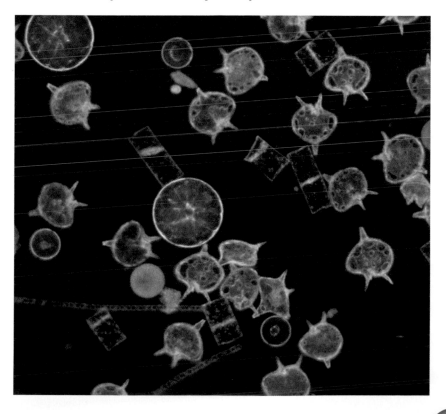

urchins wedge themselves into cracks with sturdy spines. Mussels anchor themselves by tough life-lines. A limpet's suction-cup foot clings with an iron grip that can take as much as seventy pounds of pressure to remove. And the waves slide over the curved shells of mussels and limpets without being able to get a grip.

When the waves retreat, sea snails seal the openings in their shells and barnacles close their armored tents, locking in moisture. Sea cucumbers curl into tiny, water-conserving balls. Sea anemones pull in their tentacles and collapse into blobs, covering themselves with moist mud, pebbles, and bits of shell.

There are always hungry hunters looking for a meal. Animals hide in many ways. Some, like tide pool fish, use **camouflage**. Their coloring and shape lets them blend into the environment. Clever urchins camouflage themselves—holding seaweed, pebbles, and small shells on their bodies. Some animals help each other hide. A hermit crab will allow an anemone to settle on its shell where its stinging tentacles shield the crab from attack. In return, the anemone enjoys leftovers from the crab's meals. And, when hiding does not work, crabs and sea stars will sacrifice a leg or an arm to escape a hungry predator.

Tide Pool Plants

Colorful tide pool gardens grow seaweeds. Seaweeds belong to a family of simple, plant-like organisms called algae. In the past, scientists classified algae as part of the plant kingdom. Today many scientists group algae with the protists—basic organisms that have characteristics of both plants and animals.

Seaweeds come in different colors, shapes, and sizes. There is bright green sea lettuce and rough, purple Turkish towel; spongy sea fingers and feathery mermaid's hair; tiny, yellow-brown sea bubble and large, leathery feather boa kelp.

Scientists divide the approximately ten thousand kinds of seaweeds into three main types according to their color: green seaweeds, red seaweeds, and brown seaweeds. Green seaweeds, often found in tide pools and high on the shore, are the least varied. They are usually thin, sheet-like, and bright green in color. Red seaweeds are the most plentiful and varied seaweeds. There are more than four thousand species worldwide.

Scientists divide the thousands of different kinds of seaweed into three main types: green, red, and brown.

Despite their name, red seaweeds can be red, purple, brown, or even green depending on the amount of red **pigment** they contain. Most kinds of red seaweed live in deep water; others inhabit tide pools. Brown seaweeds are the most noticeable seaweeds on the shore and are common in tide pools. Included in this group are the rockweeds and wracks and the largest of all the seaweeds—the kelps.

Long, slender surf grass also grows in tide pools. Unlike seaweeds, it is not part of the algae family. Surf grass is similar to plants that grow on land.

Seaweeds look different from the flowers, grass, and trees that grow in yards, parks, and forests. Some kinds look like splotches of color on an artist's palette or like a stiff, bristly brush. Other kinds look like wispy webs, hair, or feathers. Some are thin as paper or light and hollow like straws. Some have ragged, toothlike edges, and some have tiny bubble-shaped structures in them.

Seaweeds also feel different from land plants. Thick, springy seaweeds carpet the rocky shore. Silky seaweeds line tide pools and coat the shells of many of their inhabitants. Slippery, fringed curtains of seaweed decorate the rocks.

Seaweed and Land Plant Similarities

But seaweeds and land plants are alike in some very important ways. Both make their own food using sunlight, water, and air. This process is called photosynthesis.

In land plants, photosynthesis mainly takes place in the leaves. Land plants use chlorophyll, a green chemical found in their leaves, to capture sunlight. They use their roots to soak up water and minerals from the soil. Energy from the captured sunlight allows the water and minerals to mix with carbon dioxide, a gas from the air, to make food. The food is then carried to all parts of the plant through its stem.

Seaweeds also make their food through photosynthesis, but the process takes place in every part of the seaweed. Seaweeds contain sunlight-

Surf grass, also found in tide pools, is similar to plants that grow on land.

Seaweeds use different methods to keep from drying out during low tide.

capturing chlorophyll too. Its green color is hidden by other colored chemicals that help capture the sunlight's energy. Seaweeds use sunlight to make food from minerals and carbon dioxide found in the surrounding seawater.

Both seaweeds and land plants also have special structures or parts. Each part has a job that is important for survival. Land plants have roots to anchor them in the soil and take in water and minerals to make food. Stems hold up the plant's leaves and flowers. They carry water and minerals to "food factories" in the leaves and also carry the food to all parts of the plant. Flowers and seeds make new plants.

Seaweeds' structures are different from the structures of land plants. Holdfasts, special "grabbers"

Seaweeds use "grabbers" to attach themselves to rocks, and flexible stems to absorb pressure from waves.

that look like tangles of roots, anchor seaweeds to rocks. Flexible stems, called stipes, act like shock absorbers between the firmly fastened holdfasts and the wave-tossed tops of seaweeds. Seaweeds' often odd-shaped leaves are called blades. Blades have several important jobs. They collect light, soak up water and minerals, and support structures needed for **reproduction**. Some seaweeds also have bladders—small, air-filled floats. Bladders are like little balloons, carrying the seaweeds' blades toward the sunlight at the surface of the tide pool. Besides doing their own special jobs, all seaweed structures also carry on photosynthesis.

Seaweed Survival

Seaweeds' structures equip them to live in their watery world. Seaweeds sway in the crashing surf. They float, twist, and bend with the waves but do not break. Higher on the shore, dry, wrinkly mats of seaweed look dead. When the tide returns, they spring to life. In the rocky pools, hungry creatures search for seaweed snacks. Like the animals that live in tide pools, seaweeds have adapted to their harsh conditions.

Pounding waves batter the intertidal zone, playing tug-of-war with everything on the shore. Such force could snap a stiff stem, loosen delicate roots, and destroy tender new growth. But seaweed stipes are tough and rubbery, limp and flexible. They bend with the breaking waves. Seaweed holdfasts make a sticky glue to help them grip the rocks. The holdfasts cling so tightly that the strongest waves sometimes break off the stipes, leaving the holdfasts attached to the rocks. And, unlike land plants that grow from the top and tips of the plant, many seaweeds grow from the bottom or middle so new growth is not broken off by the crashing waves.

Seaweed can float, twist, and bend with the waves.

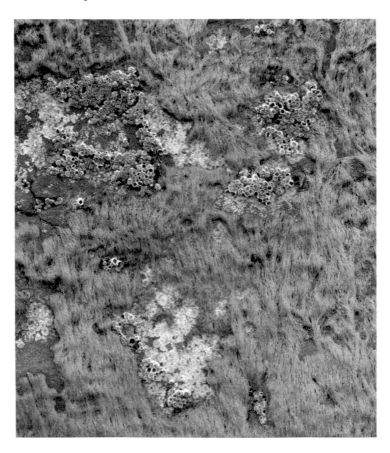

When the tide goes out or the water level in a tide pool is low, seaweeds must protect themselves from drying out. Some are coated with a layer of slimy mucus that saves moisture. Others trap moisture by collapsing into heaps. Some types grow in short, thick clumps that are more able to store moisture. Others grow in cracks, shielded from the drying sun.

Growing in seawater rich with minerals, seaweeds still need sunlight to make food. Many have developed large blades to better gather sunlight for photosynthesis. Bladders or floats help to keep seaweeds closer to the surface of the water where their blades can carry on photosynthesis more easily.

Seaweeds share their habitat with hungry herbivores. Many seaweeds are a tough meal since their leathery parts offer little nutrition to grazers looking for lunch, and this discourages other creatures from munching on them.

Homes and Food

Seaweeds are important to tide pool animals. Animals can't make their own food or oxygen. Seaweeds provide food for herbivores like sea urchins and limpets. Seaweeds also provide tide pool animals with life-giving oxygen which they make during photosynthesis.

Seaweed gardens are homes for small fish, crabs, sea stars, and other tide pool inhabitants as

Seaweeds are a source of both food and oxygen for tide pool animals.

well. Shady seaweed curtains help block out bright sunlight, which can make the water too hot for the animals that live there. To many tide pool creatures, seaweeds are also hiding places and sheltering nurseries where they lay their eggs.

Threatened Treasures

Tide pools are treasures. They are valuable sources of information about the ocean environment, a storehouse of important research resources, and a rich and remarkable habitat of their own.

The ocean covers most of our planet and makes life on earth possible by controlling the temperature of the air, supplying moisture for rainfall, and providing food, energy, minerals, and medicines. Scientists study the huge ocean using tools from computers and satellites to tide pools. Tide pools are like tiny, trapped oceans—miniature models of how an ocean environment works and stays in balance. In these miniature worlds researchers can see the daily lives of ocean animals: hunting, eating, fighting off predators, and having babies. By studying tide pools, scientists (and anyone else) can investigate the wonders of ocean life—without boats, expensive equipment, or the dangers of deep-sea diving.

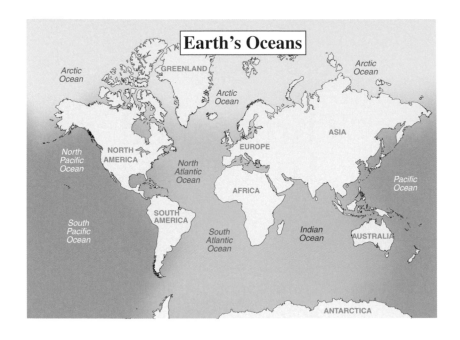

Earth's Oceans

Tide pools are also living laboratories whose inhabitants are used in environmental and human health research. Mussels are assisting scientists monitoring ocean pollution. Since pollutants become concentrated in their bodies, mussels can help scientists monitor pollution. Sea urchins are helping investigators better understand human reproduction and diseases like cancer. Sea hares are being used in important studies on human brain development, memory, and learning. "Barnacle glue" is being analyzed by dentists for its amazing strength and stickiness. Crabs, whose hard shells are actually their skeletons, may reveal how bones mend. Other **marine** organisms show promise as **antibiotics**, pain relievers, and treatments for AIDS and Alzheimer's disease.

Finally, tide pools are a unique **ecosystem** of their own. In their small, separate world, tide pool creatures have developed special ways of surviving their unusual habitat. Stranded by low tides, submerged by high tides, and pursued by land and sea hunters, tide pool animals and plants have learned to live in two worlds—on land and in the sea.

Tide Pools in Danger

Perched at the edge of the sea, tide pools are tiny worlds of their own. But they are also part of the ocean that formed them. Because of their unique position, tide pools face the threats to both these environments.

About 70 percent of the people in the United States live and work within fifty miles of the

Tide pools are living laboratories for research about health and the environment.

Seventy percent of people in the United States live and work within fifty miles of the seashore.

seashore. Refineries, power plants, hotels, resorts, parking lots, and homes crowd the coasts. Coastal development is the reason for the problems facing tide pools today—people and pollution.

Loved to Death

People love the seashore. Some visitors come to swim, surf, or picnic. Others go boating or fishing. While the rocky seashore is not the most popular place to sunbathe or picnic, it is a favorite of nature lovers who flock to easily reached tide pools to see their unusual residents up close. Every year nearly forty thousand people visit the Point Pinos tide pools located in Pacific Grove, California. Sadly, curious visitors—from beachcombers to poorly supervised school groups—often cause harm. Their careless footsteps trample hundreds of tiny animals living underfoot, and they overturn rocks and seaweed leaving creatures either to die in the hot sun, or to be eaten by predators. Sensitive animals are sometimes injured or even killed when they are plucked from the rocks, handled roughly, or moved from their homes.

Collectors also take a toll. Sightseers and beachcombers fill up their pails with sand, rocks, shells, and critters to take home as keepsakes or to add to their saltwater aquariums. **Poachers** strip certain species, such as sea urchins and some varieties of snails from the rocks, for food. Tasty abalone, once plentiful in southern California tide pools, is nearly impossible to find. A recent study suggests that the area's owl limpet population may also be declining for the same reason. Although it is illegal in most places to take tide pool dwellers as souvenirs or for food, collection still remains a serious problem. Now, even scientists must have permits to remove species for study.

Pollution Problems

Ocean pollution is another threat to tide pools. In the huge ocean, pollution is spread over a wide area. Concentrated at the coast, pollution becomes more dangerous. Ocean pollution includes litter, waste, and oil.

Human **debris** is a serious pollution problem. During the 1998 International Coastal Cleanup, a yearly event sponsored by the Center for Marine Conservation (CMC), volunteers collected more than 5.5 million pieces of trash along the U.S. coasts. Cigarette butts, plastic pieces, food bags, wrappers, paper, cans, bottles, straws, caps, and lids were part of the "dirty dozen" littering the shores.

Another pollution problem is industrial waste—chemicals used by factories and businesses in the manufacture of their products. Household chemicals and poisonous wastes from hospitals and

Volunteers collected more than five and a half million pieces of trash along U.S. coasts in 1998.

Seventy percent of marine pollution comes from land.

medical labs are also pollution dangers. The strong chemicals in fertilizers and **pesticides** used by farmers and homeowners only add to the problem.

According to the Center for Marine Conservation, marine debris comes from two sources—ocean and land. Ocean sources include fishing and pleasure boats, cargo and cruise ships, and offshore oil rigs. But 70 percent of marine debris and other pollutants come from on land. Most of it is washed off the streets. Every time it rains, street runoff carries litter, motor oil, pet wastes, and excess fertilizers and pesticides into storm drains that eventually lead to the sea. Overflowing sewer systems also carry sewage, industrial waste, and medical wastes into the ocean. Beach visitors leave behind about seventy-five tons of trash per week.

Some Solutions

Protecting tide pools means working to safeguard both the seashore and ocean environments. Federal, state, and local governments, environmental groups, and private citizens are helping with the task. Many efforts are being made—from laws to educational programs.

Collection and what scientists call the trample effect—the result of so many visitors crushing delicate tide pool organisms underfoot—are being fought in several ways. Strictly enforced laws protect tide pools. Beachcombers who take animals, plants, shells, or rocks from protected areas can be fined. Aquariums have been founded in many

Aquariums have been built in many cities to allow people to experience ocean life without harming it.

cities to offer nature lovers less harmful ways to experience ocean life, including tide pools, up close. At some, visitors can see and touch tide pool creatures in supervised areas. At others, tours of nearby tide pools educate visitors about proper tide pool conduct. Finally, Congress has established ten national seashores as part of the National Park system. Point Reyes National Seashore and Channel Islands National Park, both in California, Olympic National Park in Washington, and Acadia National Park in Maine provide protected intertidal environments. Park service rangers provide tours, and visitors can explore the tide pools, but removing anything—even a shell—is strictly forbidden.

Battling ocean pollution is everyone's responsibility. Laws like the Clean Water Act and the Marine Plastic Pollution Research and Control Act discourage water pollution. The U.S. Environmental Protection Agency (EPA), the National Oceanic and Atmospheric Administration, and the National Park Service are some of the government agencies that monitor the marine environment. Other environmental organizations sponsor important programs such as the Million Points of Blight, which aims to label a million storm drains across the country with reminders not to use them as dumping places (which eventually lead to the sea). The annual International Coastal Cleanup program gathers volunteers to collect trash that has either

Environmental organizations sponsor many programs to help educate people about how to save tide pools.

been washed up on the beach, or left by beachgoers. Recycling programs find ways to use trash to make new products, thereby reducing the amount of trash that winds up in the ocean environment. Educational programs like "Coastweeks," a yearly fall event, include a variety of activities to teach participants about coastal pollution, wildlife, and habitats. Perhaps most important in battling ocean pollution are private citizens who make the commitment not to pollute each day.

Much remains to be done to keep our seashores and their treasures—the tide pools—safe, for now and for the future.

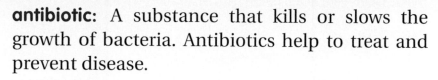

antibiotic: A substance that kills or slows the growth of bacteria. Antibiotics help to treat and prevent disease.

camouflage: The disguising of people, animals, or things in order to make them look like their surroundings

carnivore: A meat-eating animal

colony: A group of many of the same kind of animals that live together

debris: Trash or garbage

ecosystem: The plants, animals, and nonliving things that make up an environment and have an effect on each other

evaporate: To change into a vapor or gas

gravity: The natural force that causes objects to move toward the earth

habitat: The place where an animal or plant naturally lives and grows

herbivore: A plant-eating animal

inhabitant: An animal that lives in a particular place

marine: Having to do with the sea

pesticide: A chemical used to kill harmful pests, such as certain insects.

pigment: A substance in plants or animals that gives them their color

poacher: Someone who steals animals

predator: An animal that kills another animal for food

reproduction: The process by which living things produce offspring

species: A type of plant or animal

Books

Carmen Bredeson, *Tide Pools*. New York: Franklin Watts, 1999. Describes tides, tide pools, and the creatures that inhabit them.

Christine Gunzi, *Tide Pool*. New York: Dorling Kindersley, 1992. Photographs with informative labels and captions provide interesting facts about tide pools.

Anna Mearns, "Hideaway Hermits," *Ranger Rick*, July 1991. Discusses different kinds of hermit crabs, why they need shells, hermit crab predators, and hermit crab partners—animals that live in or on hermit crab shells.

Alvin and Virginia Silverstein, *Life in a Tidal Pool*. New York: Little, Brown, 1990. Offers information about tide pool animals, their characteristics, and how they interact with one another.

Websites

Center for Marine Conservation. www.cmc.org. The CMC is a nonprofit organization dedicated to protecting marine wildlife and habitats and to conserving coastal and ocean resources. This center provides important information and ways to get involved.

Enchanted Learning.
www.enchantedlearning.com.
This site covers a variety of interesting educational subjects from astronomy to explorers. The *Oceans* section includes information on tides, the intertidal zone, and tide pool animals. There are simple, labeled anatomical diagrams of many tide pool animals which can be downloaded for printing.

Monterey Bay Aquarium. www.mbayaq.org.
This aquarium is devoted to Monterey Bay, California, marine habitats—from kelp forest to sandy seafloor. Information from the Rocky Shores exhibit features facts and photos of tide pool creatures.

John G. Shedd Aquarium.
www.sheddaquarium.org.
This aquarium in Chicago exhibits more than 8,000 marine animals. The site has excellent fact sheets on a variety of tide pool species.

Virginia Institute of Marine Science.
www.vims.edu/bridge.
This site provides online resources for marine science education, including links to articles on marine invertebrates and marine pollution.

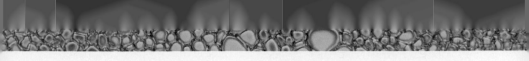

D0426488

Purchased from
Multnomah County Library
Title Wave Used Bookstore
216 NE Knott St, Portland
503-988-5021

ANIMAL CRACKERS
Circus Mayhem

First Second

Copyright © 2017 by Scott Christian Sava

Penciled digitally in Photoshop on a Cintiq 12wx display, printed out on Strathmore smooth two-ply Bristol, and touched up with Pilot Color Eno non-photo blue mechanical pencil. Inked with Sakura Micron felt tip pens sizes 02, 05 & 08. Cleanup and panel borders produced in Photoshop.

Published by First Second
First Second is an imprint of Roaring Brook Press,
a division of Holtzbrinck Publishing Holdings Limited Partnership
175 Fifth Avenue, New York, New York 10010
All rights reserved

Library of Congress Control Number: 2016942597

ISBN 978-1-62672-504-1

Our books may be purchased in bulk for promotional, educational, or business use. Please contact your local bookseller or the Macmillan Corporate and Premium Sales Department at (800) 221-7945 ext. 5442 or by e-mail at MacmillanSpecialMarkets@macmillan.com.

First edition 2017
Book design by John Green

Printed in China by Toppan Leefung Printing Ltd., Dongguan City, Guangdong Province
10 9 8 7 6 5 4 3 2 1

ANIMAL CRACKERS
CIRCUS MAYHEM

WRITTEN BY
SCOTT CHRISTIAN SAVA

ILLUSTRATED BY
MIKE HOLMES

COLOR BY
HILARY SYCAMORE

:01

First Second
New York

SHE WAS IN COMMERCIALS.

THAT JOLLY BURGER COMMERCIAL WAS ON TV FOR MONTHS.

YOU WON'T EVEN TELL ME WHERE YOU'RE GOING. WHAT'S THE BIG SECRET?

SOMETIMES GROWN-UPS HAVE THINGS THEY CAN'T SHARE WITH KIDS.

TRUST ME, SPORT, IT'S BORING ADULT STUFF.

I DON'T *WANT* TO GO TO THE CIRCUS.

C'MON, OWEN, WE'VE BEEN OVER THIS.

YOU *LOVE* ANIMALS!

THIS CIRCUS IS *FAMOUS* FOR ITS ANIMAL ACTS.

SO FAMOUS I NEVER HEARD OF IT.

HERCULES!

WHOA!!!

NOT AGAIN, CHESTERFIELD! HOW MANY TIMES DO I HAVE TO TELL YOU THAT *BALLOONS. ARE. NOT. TIRES.*

BALLOONS CAN BE ANIMALS OR AIRSHIPS OR WHOOPEE CUSHIONS OR *TIRES!*

YOU CAN LIFT A CAR!

IT WAS JUST A CLOWN CAR. TAKES MORE MUSCLE TO LIFT A *REAL* CAR.

THIS CAR IS A *CLASSIC.* MY FATHER BOUGHT IT FROM P. T. BARNUM HIMSELF!

WHATEVER YOU SAY, LITTLE MAN. I'M HAVING A TUG-O-WAR TONIGHT WITH A TRACTOR AND I NEED TO PRACTICE.

HOW ABOUT BUFFALO BOB? YOU SEE HIM? HE'S GOT FAMILY VISITING.

LAST I SAW HE WAS TALKING TO—

CAN'T A WOMAN HAVE ANY PRIVACY!! YOU CAD! THERE ARE MORE APPROPRIATE WAYS TO CALL UPON A LADY!!

IS HE ALL RIGHT?

NOT FOR LONG...

GRETCHEN! IT WAS AN ACCIDENT! THIS NEW ACT HAS ME FLYING THROUGH THE EYE OF A GIANT NEEDLE. IT'S GONNA TAKE SOME PRACTICE!

IF YOU HAD ANY *REAL* TEETH LEFT IN YOUR HEAD I'D *KNOCK THEM OUT!*

GRETCHEN! BULLET MAN! SOME CIVILITY, PLEASE! WE HAVE BUFFALO BOB'S FAMILY WITH US HERE TODAY.

FAMILY? AND WE'RE *CHOPPED LIVER?*

NICE TO MEET YOU, SON.

HI. I'M OWEN.

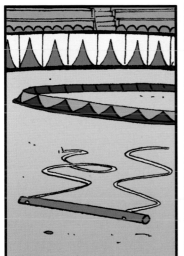

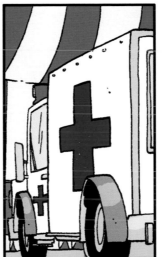

THERE, THERE, SUNSHINE. SHEMP IS GOING TO BE OKAY.

IS SHEMP OKAY?

VE'RE HOPING. VHERE IS BOB?

15

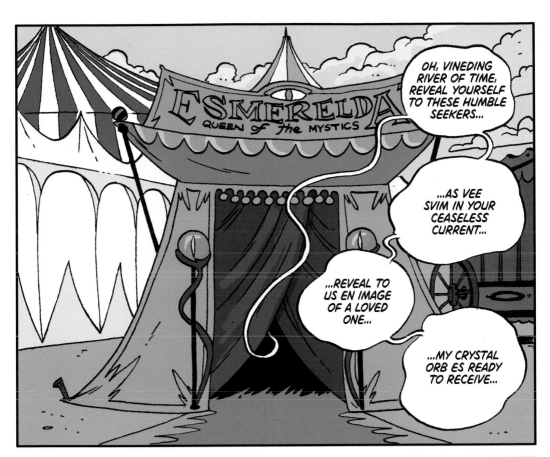

17

19

OKAY! OKAY! THE SHOW VILL GO ON BUT VEE HAVE TO ACT FAST. VULF BOY, UNCLE SAM, AND SUNSHINE: GO ENTERTAIN THE RESTLESS CROWD OUTSIDE, BUY US TIME.

OOH! I NEED TO COMB MY FACE!

APOLLO AND MAXIMUS: PULL TOGETHER A TEAM. BEFORE VEE LET ANYVUN IN I VANT A SAFETY INSPECTION. CHECK EVERY SCREW, BOLT, END LATCH. WHO KNOWS VHAT ELSE CONTORTO SABOTAGED.

YES, TALIA.

EVERYVUN ELSE PREPARE TO PERFORM BUT BE ON YOUR GUARD. CONTORTO AND HEES CREW ARE STILL AT LARGE. REPORT TO ME IF YOU SEE ENYTHING SUSPICIOUS.

ANY KVESTIONS?

WHAT ABOUT THE ANIMALS?! ISN'T THAT WHAT EVERYONE COMES TO YOUR CIRCUS TO SEE? WHY ISN'T ANYONE LOOKING FOR *THEM*?!

CHESTERFIELD VILL SEE IF HE CAN FIND SOME ENIMALS. I GO TO THE POLICE. THEY HELP LOOK FOR BOB.

OKAY, VHAT ARE YOU ALL VAITING FOR, LET'S GO!

21

HOW ABOUT I MAKE YOU A *BALLOON* ANIMAL? THAT'LL TURN YOUR FROWN UPSIDE-DOWN!

FOUND ONE ANIMAL AT LEAST!

LOOK, KID, I DON'T BLAME YA FOR BEING SORE. IF I THOUGHT I COULD TELL YA MORE I WOULD. BUT I CAN'T. BUT IT'S NOT 'CAUSE I THINK YOU'RE STUPID.

OKAY, I GET IT. YOU NEED SOME SPACE. WHY DON'T YOU STAY PUT AND I'LL GO KEEP LOOKING. YOU'LL BE SAFER HERE WITH CONTORTO ON THE LOOSE.

SAFE AND SECURE. BE BACK FOR YOU SOON.

LOCK

22

GULP

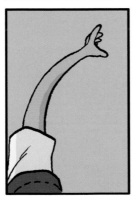

CHESTERFIELD?!

CHESTERFIELD, *HELP!*

NO WAY!

NO WAY!

NO WAY!

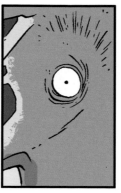

READY TO **SMASH** MY WAY OUT OF HERE!

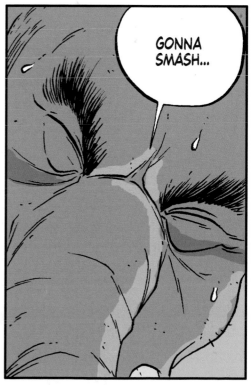

GONNA SMASH...

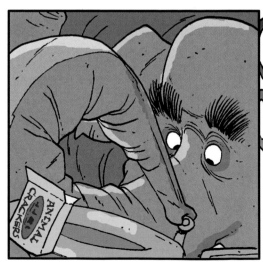

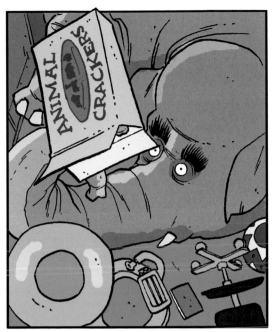

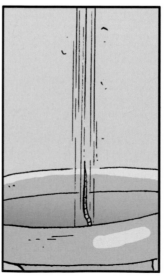

FLUMP

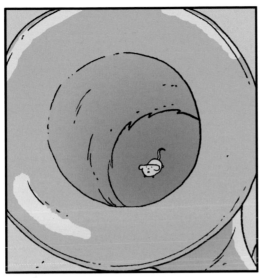
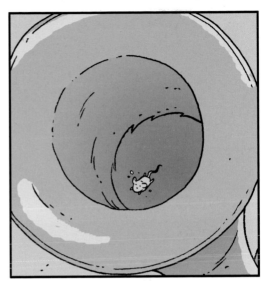

GUESS WHERE *I* AM?

BUFFALO BOB'S OFFICE! THE *LAST* PLACE THEY'D LOOK FOR ME...

CONTORTO!

BUFFALO BOB STILL WON'T TALK, HUH?

DOESN'T MATTER, THE AUDIENCE IS READY TO RIOT. THIS CIRCUS WON'T LAST ANOTHER—

NO, I DIDN'T FIND THE ANIMALS, BUT THEY CAN'T EITHER AND—

IDIOT! YOU'RE NOT LISTENING: ANIMALS GONE. BUFFALO BOB'S CIRCUS WILL SOON BE OUT OF BUSINESS. WHAT DON'T YOU UNDERSTAND?

I GOTTA GET OUT OF HERE...! I NEED TO DO SOMETHING!

VILE LITTLE RODENT!

WHERE ARE THE CRACKERS? WHERE ARE THE CRACKERS?

I WILL *SQUASH* YOU SO YOUR BRAINS COME OUT YOUR *NOSE!!*

FILTHY CREATURE, YOU CANNOT ESCAPE THE GREAT CONTORTO!!

WHAM

NO WAY I CAN REACH THAT! BUT I HAVE TO!

LITTLE STUPID RODENT— YOU CORNERED YOURSELF! NOWHERE TO GO BUT MY *STOMACH.*

THIS BETTER WORK...

BBLAPPPFFFF

FFFFFFF

WOOOO-HOOOO!

WHAHHHH
HAHHHH!

THUNK

FLUNK

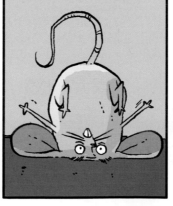

LITTLE STUPID RODENT—YOU HAVE TRAPPED YOURSELF!

=GULP=

FOUND
THE ANIMALS!
I REPEAT,
*FOUND THE
ANIMALS!*

NEED BACK-UP!
*BACK-UP
IMMEDIATELY!*

44

THEY STOPPED BOOING! I *KNEW* WE'D WIN THEM OVER!

IT'S NOT *US* THEY ARE CHEERING FOR...

LOOK! BUFFALO BOB IS BACK!

HEY, EASY!

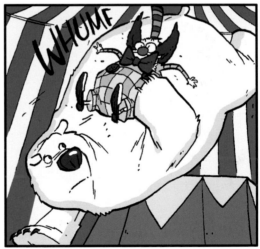

WHUMF

GOOD TO SEE YA, BOSS!

LET'S DO THE OL' POLAR BEAR PRETZEL ROUTINE AND GIVE THIS CROWD A *THRILL!*

I DON'T KNOW ANY ROUTINES....!

WHAT DO YA MEAN, YA DON'T KNOW? WE DONE IT A MILLION TIMES!

45

I'M NOT UNCLE BOB!

WHA— *JEEZ!* WELL, DO **SOMETHING!** WE CAN'T JUST KEEP RUNNING IN CIRCLES. THIS IS A TOUGH CROWD!

SOMETHING, YEAH...

ROAR!!

THIS ISN'T PART OF THE ACT!

WHAT THE—

EL GATO GRANDE!!!

HAVE NO FEAR, *BULLET MAN* IS HERE!

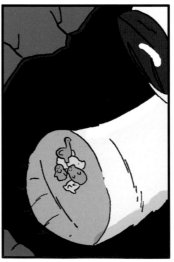

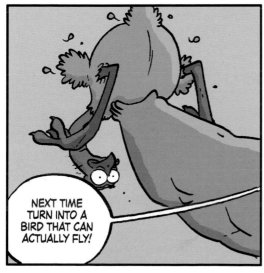

50

ARGHHHHHH!!

HA!
I SHOULD
HAVE WON A *BIG*
STUFFED ANIMAL
FOR THAT
TOSS!

HURRY! HERE COMES CONTORTO...

CRA-THUNK

...AND A *CAR!!!*

¡UN GATO SIEMPRE CAE EN SUS PIES!

HISSSS!

CATS ALSO HATE WATER!

YOU FOUL EXCUSE FOR A FOWL!

Whipp Whipp

Leap!

BOING

GOOD DAY FOR A RIDE!

FLUMP!

I WILL CARVE YOU UP. THEN I WILL FIND THAT BEAR AND MAKE A RUG OUT OF HIM!

THEN I WILL FIND THAT ILLUSIONIST THAT CAN TURN ONE ANIMAL INTO ANOTHER!

THAT SECRET WILL BE *MINE!*

GAD ZEUS... FELLED BY A CHEAP SHOT...

CAN'T CLUB WHAT YOU CAN'T SEE!

GRETCHEN!

GRUNT!

TOSS

GRUNT!

CONK!

I'M READY FOR YOU NOW, YOU NEANDERTHAL-BRAINED NINNY!

YOU WANT THIS WRECK AS YOUR COFFIN?

≥GULP≤

58

WELCOME TO THE ACT...

BECAUSE OF YOU...

SWOOOSH

...WE ARE MISSING OUR THIRD.

WE JUST HEARD WORD OUR BROTHER SHEMP WILL BE OKAY AND HOME SOON...

CRACK

HIS ROOM IN THE HOSPITAL IS NOW AVAILABLE.

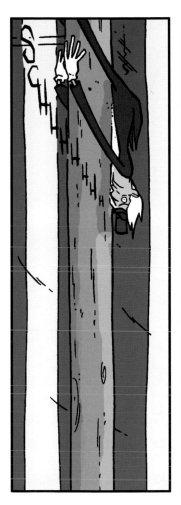

60

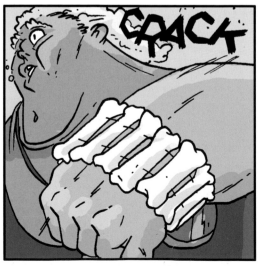

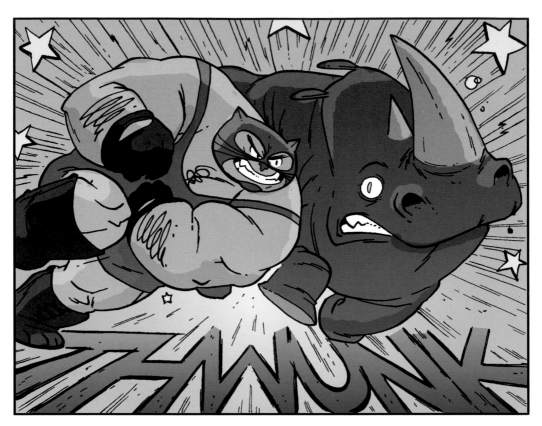

¡¡ANIMAL DE CIRCO ESCUCHIMIZADO!! ¡YO TE LEVANTO COMO UNA PLUMA!

¡UN NUEVO ACTO! ¡"EL RINOCERONTE VOLADOR"!

¡¡EL ACTO FINAL!!

¡AL BATE, MI AMIGA!

GRUNT?

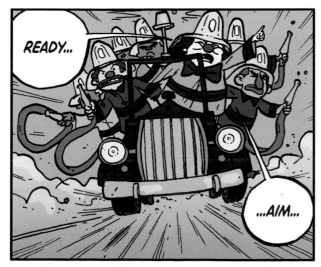

READY...

...AIM...

...FIRE!

SHRUSSH

GRACIAS,
CROOGA.
AHORA VAMOS
A ACABAR CON
ELLOS.

GRUNT!

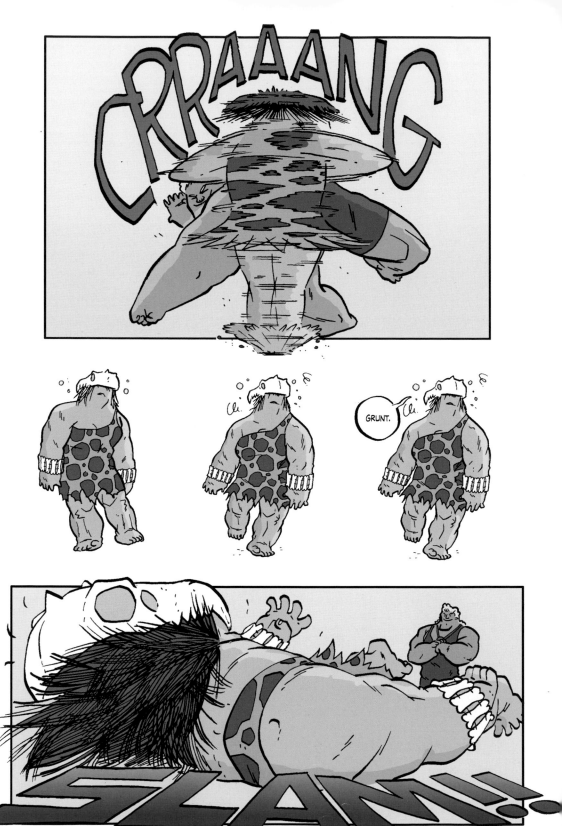

¡AY CARAMBA!

THREE AGAINST ONE, EL GATO GRANDE!

MAKE THAT FOUR.

MAKE THAT SIX.

MAKE THAT... MAKE THAT A LOT!

WOOT! WOOT!

YAY!

BEST SHOW ON EARTH!

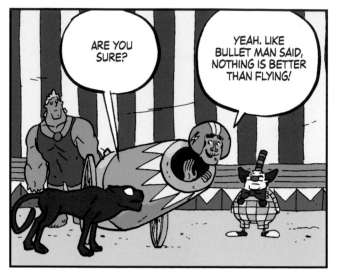

ARE YOU SURE?

YEAH. LIKE BULLET MAN SAID, NOTHING IS BETTER THAN FLYING!

THEN HURRY AND SAVE THE MAN I LOVE.

LIGHT THE FUSE!

FSSHHHT

tzizzle

tzizzle

BLAM

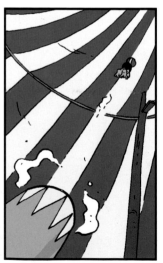

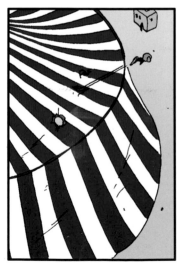

77

THAT... HURT.

NO VAN. AM I TOO LATE?

VREEEM

ERRT

THEY THOUGHT THEY COULD HOLD ME!!

ME!!

THE GREAT CONTORTO!

THE *GREATEST* ESCAPE ARTIST OF—

FIRST I CAN'T FIND ANY OF YOUR FILTHY ANIMALS AND NOW THEY WON'T LEAVE ME ALONE!

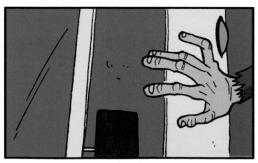

THE BOY! I HAVE FOUND THE BOY!!

WHAT HAPPENED...?

TAKE IT EASY, SON...YOU... UM...AH...YOU GOT KIDNAPPED BY SOME RUFFIANS...

YOU'RE SAFE NOW, KID.

BUT...I WAS AN ANIMAL... I MEAN, MANY ANIMALS... I MEAN...

I DON'T UNDERSTAND... IT WAS SO REAL... THERE WERE THESE ANIMA—

I THINK YOU GOT CONKED A LITTLE TOO HARD ON THE HEAD, M'BOY.

89